Word Check:
Using Words Correctly

A concise *Word Check* of over 500 words most
frequently used incorrectly: imposter words, two-
timing words, hidden-trap words, look-alikes and
grammatical mischief-makers. Authoritative,
practical and witty, *Word Check* is your guide
through the minefield of those words we are never
quite sure about.

The **One Hour Wordpower** *series*

WORD BANK
Expanding Your Vocabulary
WORD CHECK
Using Words Correctly
GOOD GRAMMAR IN ONE HOUR
THE NAME BOOK
THE SECRETS OF SPEED READING
GUIDE TO WORDPLAY AND WORD GAMES
CRISP CLEAR WRITING IN ONE HOUR
SPELL CHECK
1000 Most Misspelled Words

RADIO DETECTIVE
John Escott

A piece of amazing deduction by the Roundbay Radio Detective when Donald, the radio's young presenter, solves a mystery but finds out more than anyone expects.

RAGDOLLY ANNA'S CIRCUS
Jean Kenward

Made only from a morsel of this and a tatter of that, Ragdolly Anna is a very special doll and the six stories in this book are all about her adventures.

SEE YOU AT THE MATCH
Margaret Joy

Six delightful stories about football. Whether spectator, player, winner or loser these short, easy stories for young readers are a must for all football fans.

One Hour Wordpower

Word Check:
Using Words Correctly

GRAHAM KING

Mandarin
in association with
The Sunday Times

A Mandarin Paperback
WORD CHECK

First published in Great Britain 1993
by Mandarin Paperbacks
an imprint of Reed Consumer Books Ltd
Michelin House, 81 Fulham Road, London SW3 6RB
and Auckland, Melbourne, Singapore and Toronto

A CIP catalogue record for this title
is available from the British Library
ISBN 0 7493 1522 9

Printed and bound in Great Britain
by Cox & Wyman Ltd, Reading, Berks

Acknowledgements

The following works provided the definitive sources for meanings and usage in *Word Check*:

The Oxford English Dictionary, Webster's New Twentieth Century Dictionary, Cassell's English Dictionary, Collins English Dictionary, Longman New Generation Dictionary, The Encyclopaedia Britannica, Fontana Dictionary of Modern Thought. Also Fowler's *A Dictionary of Modern English Usage*, Eric Partridge's *Usage and Abusage*, Harry Shaw's *Dictionary of Problem Words and Expressions*, John Bremner's *Words on Words*, Alexander Witherspoon's *Common Errors in English* and William Safire's *On Language* and *What's The Good Word?*

Introduction

If we are what we say and write, what are we to make of the author of this?

> 'Reference your contract proposal we except all those items within the parameters we discussed, but its neither fair or acceptable to insist on a delivery date prior to April. We could have had agreement months ago if you had not made the order dependant on such unrealistic delivery dates.'

The paragraph contains five examples of words used incorrectly, and a further example of indecorous usage.* It is taken from a letter written (or dictated) by a young middle-management sales executive of a London firm **which** (not **that**) supplies industrial cleaning materials.

But before we start gleefully gloating over the young man's linguistic lapses, we might be wise to ensure our own houses are in order. Are we all confident about using **lay** and **lie**, **who** and **whom**, **shall** and **will**, **that** and **which**, **its** and **it's**? Is it **try and** or **try to**? **Compare to** or **compare with**?

Are the kids **noisy** or **noisome**? Is petrol **flammable** or **inflammable**? What's the difference between **manslaughter** and **murder**? **Perennial** and **annual**? **Peremptory** and **perfunctory**? **Perspicacity** and **perspicuity**?

Does it really matter? Well, a man who confuses **prostrate** with **prostate** is just as likely to knock on the door of a **proctor** as a **proctologist**. Apart from being downright embarrassing, using words incorrectly

---

All the answers will be found in this book.

can transform what you say, write and mean into garbage and gobbledegook.

Few of us are ever free from doubts over the proper use of words. Many of us go through life blithely unaware that we are using certain words or expressions wrongly, and feel puzzled and resentful when we are misunderstood.

It need be neither difficult nor time-consuming to improve our understanding and use of 'difficult', look-alike and chronically misused words. The aim of *Word Check* is to provide the means to achieve this, concisely and invitingly. Many of the black holes in our usage of certain words arise from complex rules; in this book, however, you will search in vain for these, as you will for terms such as predicate nominative complement and non-restrictive personal relative pronoun.

Word Check will relieve anxieties about **among** and **amongst**, **hiccup** and **hiccough**, **on** and **upon**. It will explain the subtle differences between **obsolete** and **obsolescent**, **obligate** and **oblige**, **relatively** and **comparatively**. It will explain the true meanings of **burgeoning**, **decimate**, **empathy** and **quantum leap**. It will introduce you to the Hemingway mnemonic to help you choose between **who** and **whom**. And it will gently lead you away from clichés and vogue words like **hopefully**, **viable**, **debrief** and **utilise**. Browse through this book with pleasure; refer to it for ever (not **forever**).

Word Check

a, an

Use **a** before words beginning with consonants (a book, a glass, a TV) and **an** before words beginning with vowels (an apple, an egg, an ice-cream, an omelette, an undertaker). There are some exceptions, however: the word one, because of the way it is pronounced, demands an **a** (a one-horse town); words beginning with a soft h need an **an** (an heiress, an habitual liar) but words that sound the h don't (a horse, a hospital, a hotel); and certain words beginning with the long u which is pronounced 'yew' need an **a** (a ukelele, a uniform).

accent, dialect

An **accent** is a variation of pronunciation from the standard language; a **dialect** also strays from standard pronunciation but in addition uses a different vocabulary and grammar.

accept, except

To **accept** is to receive something; **except** means to exclude, omit, leave out, reject.

accident, injury

An **accident** is an unforeseen event but which need not necessarily result in **injury**: 'It was a spectacular accident and it was amazing that nobody was injured.'

actually, virtually, really

Actually and **really** mean in fact, but both words are much abused and over-used. 'Did he actually say that?' is legitimate; 'Well, actually, I wouldn't mind a drink' is abuse. **Virtually** means in effect,

9

substantially, mostly, for all practical purposes, not quite.

advantage, benefit

An **advantage** is a situation that favours success; a **benefit** is a form of help that is earned, paid for or given.

adversary, opponent

Both are interchangeable, a fine difference being that **adversary** has a hostile and antagonistic ring to it, while **opponent** has sportier, friendlier connotations.

adverse, averse

They look and sound similar but are used in very different ways. **Adverse** means hostile and damaging: 'The adverse conditions wrecked their holiday.' **Averse** indicates disinclination and reluctance: 'She is averse to dishing out favours.'

affect, effect

These two words have a profusion of meanings that produce a rash of confusions! To **affect** is to influence or to cause something to happen: 'Smoking can adversely affect your health.' An **effect** is a result: 'One effect of smoking is lung cancer.' Other meanings are close, but not the same: 'The burglar effected entry by the skylight'; 'The third movement of the symphony always affected him greatly.' Remember that:

- **affect** – cause – usually a verb
- **effect** – result – usually a noun

affecting, affection, affectation

A troublesome trio! An **affecting** play is one that touches the emotions; **affection** describes the act or state of fondness and attachment; while an **affectation** is a pretence.

after, afterwards

'He ran after the robber' means to pursue or seek, but **after**, like **afterwards** (and **afterward** – American) also means following in order or later in time. **Afters** are desserts or puddings.

aggravate, exasperate

Aggravate means to make a condition worse; it does not mean to annoy. If you want to **exasperate** someone, try teasing, irritating or provoking them, which could **aggravate** their ill-temper.

agree with, agree to

One usually **agrees with** a person but **agrees to** a proposition or an idea. 'I agreed with him about using the car but couldn't agree to his taking it for a week.'

A letter or two is all it takes

A changed letter in a word can make a lot of difference, and most of us make malapropian slips from time to time. Witness these:

- He's in hospital in the expensive care ward
- When it comes to marriage, Western people believe in the principle of monotony
- She went off in high dungeon
- He was proud to have at last entered the portholes of fame
- Although he's old he still has all his facilities
- Superman was supposed to have had X-rated vision

---

all right

If we accept **already, altogether** and **almost**, why not **alright**? Sorry, **alright** is all wrong, and although you'll see it in countless novels and magazine articles the authorities insist it doesn't exist.

alter, altar

As the builder said to the bishop: 'I'm sorry, but I can't alter the altar.'

alternate, alternative

Alternate means one after the other, to take turns or to substitute. An **alternative** is a choice, usually restricted to only one other option. The same applies to **alternately** and **alternatively**. 'You can work alternately, that is on alternate days, or alternatively you might prefer to work one week on and one week off.'

America, American

What is **America**? Does it mean North America, including Canada; or the Americas, which might include Central America, the Caribbean and even South America? Do **Americans** include native Indians and Nicaraguans along with citizens of the Bronx and Brooklyn? The sheer weight of usage now defines **America** as the **United States of America**, and **Americans** as citizens of that nation, and it's bad luck for the rest. If you wish to be both clear and fair, use the **United States**, the **United States of America**, the **USA** or the **US**. Where the term **US citizen** is cumbersome, there is little alternative but to use **American**: 'The current record is held by an American.'

although, though

Fairly interchangeable. **Though** means 'despite the fact that . . .'; **although** means 'even though'. It's a matter of what looks and sounds right: 'Although it was a mongrel, I bought the dog anyway'; 'I bought the dog, though it was a mongrel.'

amateur, novice

An **amateur**, as opposed to a **professional**, indulges in an activity as a pastime. A **novice** is a beginner, while a **tyro**, a word rarely used now, is an awkward, untrained novice.

American English

Most of us are familiar with those words that in the US have different spellings than they have in Britain: **tire/tyre, sulfur/sulphur, center/centre, color/colour** and so on. Americans also use different words to describe similar things: **elevator/lift, vacation/holiday, sidewalk/footpath, diaper/nappie, candy/sweets** are just a few. No offence or embarrassment is caused if we get these wrong, but watch out for words like **fanny** (which denotes two completely different parts of the anatomy), **pecker** (Americans have been known to fall down in shock when exhorted to 'keep your pecker up'), and **knock up**, which can have the same effect when, for example, a hotel receptionist is asked for an early morning call: 'Can you knock me up at half past six?'

---

among, amongst, between

Use **between** to connect two persons, objects or ideas: 'There is little difference between the two of them.' **Among** is used in connection with several things: 'There is little difference among all five candidates.' **Amongst** means the same, but why not use the shorter, simpler **among**?

amoral, immoral

Amoral means unconcerned with morals, an unmoral person, someone without a moral code. To be **immoral** is to act against a moral code, to be licentious, to offend an existing moral code.

analysis, synthesis

Analysis is to take apart, to examine, to reduce something to its elements; **synthesis** is the opposite, to put things together, to combine, to build something from various elements.

anticipate, expect, hope

The traditional meaning of **anticipate** is foresee or 'think of beforehand': 'He anticipated the cyclone by putting into the nearest harbour.' Many people mistakenly use **anticipate** for **expect**, which means to look forward to something that is certain or very likely: 'I expect you to be in early on Mondays.' It is interesting that Nelson exhorted his men with 'England expects . . .' rather than 'England hopes . . .'; **hope** is an altogether more wishy word meaning to desire something with confidence but with an uncertain expectation of fulfilment: 'I hope the neighbour's party won't be too noisy.'

anxious, eager

'She was anxious to get home' is wrong; what is probably meant is, 'She was anxious (about walking in the dark) and eager to get home.'

Anxious implies a degree of fear or apprehension, while to be **eager** is to be impatient, keen, enthusiastic.

anybody, anyone

These are interchangeable, and singular. 'If anybody/anyone is there, will he please answer the doorbell?' is correct. However, with objections nowadays to the 'he', and with the questioner not knowing the gender of the person on the other side of the door, it is now acceptable to use 'they' or 'their': 'Will they please answer the doorbell?' **Anyone** is split into two words when single persons or objects are being described: 'Anyone can eat any one of these cakes.'

any more

Try saying **anyway, anyhow, anyone, anything**; now say, 'He doesn't live here anymore'. It comes out as two words, doesn't it, with the stress on 'more'? That's why there is no such word as 'anymore'. So don't write it that way any more.

apparent, evident

Apparent means seeming to appear; **evident** means conclusive, clear to one's understanding. **Manifest** is the strongest term, which means clear to both sight and understanding.

appraise, apprise, assess, evaluate

To **appraise** is to estimate the worth of somebody or something; to **assess** is to estimate the value of something, usually property, for tax purposes; to **evaluate** is to determine the numerical and monetary value of something; to **apprise** is to inform: 'The waiter quietly apprised him of the size of the bill.'

around, round, about

Using these words is largely a matter of taste. 'I
have **about** 100 LPs in my collection' is usually
preferred to **around**, and 'I walked **round** the city'
is preferable to **around**.

assume, presume

One meaning of **assume** is unambiguous: to
undertake something, as in, 'He arrogantly
assumed the role of leader.' The other meaning,
to suppose, to take for granted, is often confused
with **presume**, which means to take for granted
without any reasoning or proof. Should Stanley
have said, 'Dr Livingstone, I assume?' A fine
difference.

assurance, insurance

Assurance is life insurance in the form of a policy
that assures an eventual financial benefit.
Insurance is a guarantee of payment for damage
through fire, accident or some form of
misfortune.

assure, ensure, insure

To **assure** somebody is to give them confidence;
to **ensure** is to make certain; to **insure** is to
protect financially.

authentic, genuine

Authentic is usually applied to something that is
produced by someone, about which there is no
doubt; it is the opposite of **counterfeit**: 'The
expert agreed that the painting was an authentic
Goya.' **Genuine** has a wider range of meanings
and is generally used to imply some innate or
original quality: 'The handbag was genuine
leather.'

average, ordinary

To say someone lives in an **average** home is meaningless; the person lives in an **ordinary** home. **Average** should only be used in its mathematical sense and even then there can be different meanings. If five individuals are aged 5, 11, 14, 20 and 25, their **average** (mean) age is the total 75 divided by the number 5 = 15.

back, behind, backward, backwards

Back is a true all-purpose word describing a position at the rear, away from you, reversed or returning, and, with its other meanings, is used in an amazing number of ways (**quarterback, backchat, backslider, back-seat driver**). But if we say '**in front of**', why can't we say '**in back of**' like the Americans? Well, it isn't done in Britain, where we say **behind. Backward** is an adjective: 'He was a backward child'; 'It was a backward step'; but it can also be used adverbially along with **backwards**. As adverbs, either **backward** or **backwards** may be used: 'He stepped backward/backwards.'

baited, bated

Bated means restrained or diminished; **bait** is food used as a lure to catch something: 'He stood there with bated breath while his wife baited the hook.'

balcony, circle, dress circle, gallery, stalls

In most theatres, the **stalls** are at floor level, with the **circle**, usually divided into **dress circle** and **upper circle**, on the next level. Above the circle is the **balcony**, with the **gallery** at the very top.

baring, barring, bearing

These derive from **bare**, **bar** and **bear**, meaning respectively: to uncover, to obstruct, and to carry.

because, since, on account of, owing to, due to

Some tough decision-making here! **Because** means 'for the reason'; **because of** means 'by reason of': 'He had to buy a new car because the other one packed up'; 'He had to return his new car because of a faulty gear box'. **On account of** is used to qualify a phrase: 'He can't drive the car on account of the gear box.' Use **since** to imply a time lapse: 'He's been walking to work since his car broke down.' **Owing to, on account of** and **because of** are for all practical purposes synonymous; the odd man out is **due to** which strictly speaking means **caused by** and should always link the result with the cause: 'His failure with girls was due to not having a car.' Careful users will not use **due to** as a substitute for **because**.

begin, commence, initiate, start

Although these words have much the same meaning, they are used differently. **Initiate** and **inaugurate** are mostly used to describe the origination of a specific undertaking, like a building project or the foundation of an association. **Commence** is interchangeable with **begin**, except that it is rather more formal, while **start** implies a certain abruptness: 'Drivers, start your engines!'

believe, feel, think

The usage of these words follows this logic: you **believe** with faith, you **feel** with your senses and emotions, and you **think** with your mind: 'I believed he was telling the truth but felt he was hiding something, and I now think he was lying all the time.'

beneath, under

Beneath and **below** mean 'lower than' and are the opposite of **above**; they all describe a position but without reference to any scale. **Under** (and **underneath**) is the opposite of **over** and both suggest a sense of position and proximity: 'His exam marks were well below mine'; 'She slid eagerly under the blankets.' As you can see, the differences are extremely subtle.

benefit

See **advantage, benefit**

beside, besides

Beside means next to, or by the side of. **Besides** means in addition to, or moreover: 'She wanted me to sit beside her; besides, there were no other vacant seats in the room.'

between

See **among, amongst, between**

biannual, biennial

Biannual is twice a year; **biennial** is once very two years. What, then, is **bi-monthly**? The answer could be either twice a month or once every two months, so it should be avoided. Instead be specific and use twice-monthly, six times yearly, once every two months, etc.

Bible, bible

When referring to the Old and New Testaments, use a capital B, but use a lower case b in the context of, for example, 'His book on stamp collecting is regarded as the bible of philately.'

billion

It is well known that the **US billion** is a thousand million, and that the **British billion** is a million million. Unfortunately this considerable distinction escapes the media and financial institutions so that we now have, in Britain, a situation where much of the time a billion means a thousand million. To avoid ambiguity, say or write 1400 million, not 1.4 or 0.0014 billion.

blond, blonde

This may come as a surprise to many, but **blond** is used in the masculine context, and **blonde** in the feminine.

born, borne, bourne

'He was born on September 1, having been borne by his mother for the full nine months.' **Bourne** is an old English word for a stream that survives in place names such as Littlebourne, Bishopsbourne, etc.

both, each

Both embraces two things while **each** refers to one of two or more things: 'Both buckets had holes in them'; 'each of the three buckets was riddled with holes'.

bravery, bravado, bravura, courage, heroism

Bravery is the readiness to face danger or pain; **bravado** is the ostentatious pretence of bravery; **bravura** is a display of daring brilliance, often in an artistic performance. **Courage** is the quality required to meet confrontation or danger with firm resolve – a quality we'd all like to possess at times of stress or challenge. **Heroism** implies an act of selflessness that transcends normal human behaviour.

breach, breech

To **breach** is to break or violate, as in a breach (break or gap) in the wall; a breach (violation) of the peace. **Breech** (remember that breeches are the garment that covers the posterior) is the rear part of anything, as in breech birth.

Britain

Britain and Great Britain are synonymous, and mean the union of England, Scotland and Wales. The United Kingdom (full title: The United Kingdom of Great Britain and Northern Ireland, abbreviated to the UK) comprises England, Scotland, Wales and Northern Ireland. The British Isles include the UK, the dependencies of the Isle of Man and the Channel Islands.

broach, brooch

To **broach** is to open up: 'He eventually broached the delicate subject of marriage.' A **brooch** is jewellery, usually fixed to the clothing with a pin.

burgeon, burgeoning

Often used incorrectly, to mean growing or swelling. What it really means is something that's *starting* to grow, or sprouting.

burglary, robbery, stealing, theft

Stealing is to take or appropriate something belonging to someone else, without their permission. **Burglary** is entering premises with intent to steal or commit a felony. **Robbery** is stealing that involves violence or the threat of it. **Theft** is synonymous with stealing.

callous, callus

Callous is used to denote insensitivity in people: 'He was callous towards his animals.' A **callus** is a patch of hard skin.

can, may, might

Can and **may** each have two meanings. The first relates to possibility: 'I can go to the party (now that I've finished my chores)'; 'I may go to the party (if I feel well enough).' The second relates to permission, and in this context any difference between **can** and **may** is virtually extinct: 'Yes, you can go to the party'; 'Yes, you may go to the party.' Much the same applies to **could** and **might**: 'Could/might I go to the party?'; but **can't** has completely replaced **mayn't**.

capital, capitol

The **capitol** is the legislative building, while the **capital** is the city in which the legislature is situated. The Capitol in Washington DC always has a capital C.

casual, causal

A confusing pair of near opposites. **Casual** denotes accidental, unplanned, a chance happening, relaxed. **Causal** is the relationship between an effect and its cause: 'The causal element in their break-up was his casual attitude to money, and the lack of it.'

catholic, Catholic

With a small c, **catholic** means wide-ranging, comprehensive, near-universal: 'He had catholic tastes in music.' With a capital C, it is the shortened form for the Roman Catholic religion.

cavalry, Calvary

Cavalry are mounted soldiers, on horses, camels or wheels; **Calvary** is the mount near Jerusalem where Christ was crucified.

celibate, chaste

To be **chaste** is to be pure, modest, and sexually faithful. To be **celibate** is to abstain from marriage (and sexual intercourse) altogether, as with the members of many religious orders.

centre, middle

The **centre** of something is geometrically precise and measurable; the **middle** of something is a more general, approximate term.

Christian name, first name, given name

Be careful of using the term **Christian name** loosely; strictly speaking, the term should be used only when referring to the first or given names of Christians. The other terms are safer.

chronic, acute

Acute means sharp and quick, whereas **chronic** means almost the opposite, long lasting and recurring: 'The acute pains he suffered were symptoms of a chronic illness.'

claim, allege, assert, maintain

Just four of a group of words that are often used synonymously and wrongly. To **claim** is to demand or assert a right: 'He came to England to claim the crown.' It is, however, often used wrongly as a synonym for **declare, assert, protest** and **allege**. To **allege** is to assert without proof, and as it nowadays implies guilt should be used with caution: 'the alleged bribe'; 'the alleged crime'. **Assert** is stronger than **said** and means to declare positively. The primary meanings of

23

maintain are **hold**, **preserve** and **sustain**, so it is a supportive word: 'In the face of the allegations she maintained her innocence.'

climactic, climatic, climacteric

'The climatic conditions were almost unbearable' disposes of that one. **Climactic** relates to a climax, a high point, while a **climacteric** is a critical period in life, most usually the male or female menopause.

colony, protectorate, dependency

A **colony** is a territory annexed by another power; once numbering over a hundred, only a few of these now survive. These include former British Crown Colonies, now termed **dependencies**, which have their own legislatures – Belize, Cayman Islands, the Falklands and Hong Kong (until 1997) are examples. A **protectorate** is a territory protected and defended by a stronger state.

commonly, customarily, frequently, generally, habitually, ordinarily, usually

Commonly, **generally**, **ordinarily** and **usually** are virtually synonymous, meaning 'normally as expected'. **Customarily** differs by only a fine degree, meaning 'according to established practice'. **Frequently** means often, while **habitually** implies frequency as the result of habit.

compare to, compare with

These are a troubling pair but it is usually accepted that **compared to** is used to express dissimilarities to make a point: 'She often compared her boyfriend's intelligence to two thick planks.' **Compared with** is used to note the differences between two similar things: 'You can't really compare Caruso's voice with Pavarotti's.'

compose, comprise, constitute

Comprise is the odd man out and means 'consists of': 'The building comprises seven rooms and the usual offices.' It is a formal word that's falling out of use. The meanings of **compose** and **constitute** are similar – to form, or to make up: 'The pudding is composed of some weird ingredients'; 'She hardly dared list the ingredients that constituted the pudding.'

complement, compliment, supplement

A **complement** is that which makes something complete: 'The hospital finally had its full complement of nurses.' A **compliment** is an expression of praise, and a **supplement** is an addition to something already complete. They are also used as verbs: 'She complemented the dish with a swirl of cream and a cherry'; 'He complimented her on the meal'; 'The doctor supplemented her diet with a course of vitamins and minerals.'

concede, accede

Accede implies willing agreement, while **concede** implies grudging agreement or giving way: 'He conceded the argument to his opponent'; 'He acceded enthusiastically to the idea of a return match.'

conscience, conscious, conscientious

A **conscience** is a person's sense of what is right and wrong. **Conscious** implies self-awareness, being aware of one's mental and physical state. To be **conscientious** is to act according to a code of principles.

consecutive, successive

Consecutive means following without an interval or break, while successive means following in order but without emphasis on the intervals. If jockey Lester Piggott had won nine consecutive Derbys he would have won the nine races over nine years; in fact he has won nine successive Derbys over 35 years.

consensus

A consensus is an agreement of opinion, so the cliché 'consensus of opinion' is to be avoided.

conservative, Conservative

With the small c it means opposed to change, moderate, cautious and conventional; with a capital C it means a member or supporter of a Conservative political party.

consultant, specialist

In medical parlance, patients are referred to a specialist, while a consultant is a specialist who is consulted by doctors.

continual, continuous

Continual means repeated at short intervals; continuous means uninterrupted.

converse, inverse, obverse, reverse

Of this quartet, all meaning opposite in some sense, inverse and obverse can be ignored unless you have a need for them – for example in coin collecting or mathematics. Converse and conversely (which is used loosely as 'on the other hand') denote a reversal of meaning: 'Every journalist knows that dog bites man – and its converse, man bites dog.' Note also that to converse means to have a conversation. Reverse is rarely misunderstood: 'He states that a fibre diet makes you fat; actually, the reverse is true.'

Contradictory words

When you **dust** an object, do you clean it of dust, or sprinkle fine powder on it? Why does a **seeded** bun have seeds baked on it, while **seeded** raisins have the seeds taken out? Does a child know the difference between **getting up** from the table, and **getting down**? These two-way words and terms are understandably the source of much confusion. Try looking up **ravel** and **unravel** in the dictionary: they can both mean the same. And **parboil**, a model of imprecision, means both to boil thoroughly, and to boil partially.

convince, persuade

Convince implies proving something to somebody by argument, by an exposition of the facts, while **persuade** suggests winning over someone to a point of view by appealing to reason or the emotions.

copy

See **replica, copy, facsimile**

correspond to, correspond with

If you **correspond with** someone, you exchange letters with them. **Correspond to** means to be in harmony with, or to tally with: 'Your version of the affair corresponds to that of Matilda's.' Don't get confused with **correspondent** (one who writes letters) and **co-respondent** (someone cited as 'the other party' in divorce proceedings).

couple, pair

A **couple** is two things that are united or joined together, as in a couple of drinks or a married couple. A **pair** is two things of a kind that are mutually dependent, as in a **pair** of scissors (joined) and a pair of gloves (not joined).

courage

See **bravery, bravado, bravura, courage, heroism**

curb, kerb

Curb means to check or restrain; **kerb** is the edge of the pavement, the drop between paved footpath and gutter. In the US they say the **curb** is the edge of the pavement.

currant, current

A **currant** is a small, dark, dried grape. **Current** has two meanings: a flow (of electricity, water, air); and existing in the present time: 'It is difficult to keep up with current events.'

cyclone, hurricane, tornado, typhoon

A **hurricane** is a violent gale with winds exceeding 75 miles an hour; a **cyclone** is a hurricane, the winds of which blow spirally towards a region of low barometric pressure. **Tornados** and **typhoons** are hurricane winds that rotate, creating funnel or cylindrical shapes.

cynical, sceptical

A **cynic** is someone who believes there is little good in anyone or anything; a **sceptic** is a doubter who has a problem believing anything without ample proof.

dais, lectern, podium, rostrum

A **rostrum** is a raised platform, and a **dais** is a rostrum on which several people can sit or stand.

A **podium** is a platform for a single speaker. A **lectern** is the stand on which the speaker props his notes.

The death watch

Watch out for the family of death words as they can spring unpleasant surprises.
Deadly can mean fatal, poisonous, relentless or even deadly boring; while **deathly** means 'like death': 'Her face was deathly pale.'
Deathless means immortal; its use today is almost always satirical, as in 'deathless prose'. **Deceased** is perfectly correct even though it is mostly used as a euphemism for **dead**; interestingly, animals are dead, never deceased.

---

debar, disbar

Debar means to exclude or to shut out; **disbar** means to expel, usually from a law court.

deceitful, deceptive

To be **deceitful** is to deliberately mislead or cheat. **Deceptive** describes the effect of a misleading circumstance: 'The bright sunshine proved deceptive, for it was really quite cold.'

decent, descent, dissent

Decent means good, respectable, morally upright; **descent** is a movement downwards; **dissent** is disagreement. Note also the spelling of the opposites, **ascent** and **assent**.

decimate

Used widely to indicate great destruction and even total annihilation, its true meaning is to destroy

one in ten – originally Roman legionnaires. Use
carefully.

defuse, diffuse

Defuse means to remove a device or some
circumstance likely to cause an explosion or an
explosive situation. **Diffuse** means to spread:
'Unrest was diffused among the crowd, and he
knew he had to defuse what was becoming an
ugly situation.'

dependant, dependent

The difference here is that **dependant** is a noun
and **dependent** is an adjective; a **dependant** is
someone **dependent** upon some form of physical,
moral or financial support: 'It was well known that
the captain had half a dozen dependants in various
ports'; 'The young man was unfortunately
dependent on drugs.'

dependency

See **colony, dependency, protectorate**

deprecate, depreciate

To **deprecate** is to express disapproval while
depreciate means to lower in value: 'The value
of his holdings had depreciated by half.'

desire, want, need

Of this trio, **need** expresses the strongest
requirement and urgency. **Want** implies a less
urgent craving, while **desire** involves a degree of
wishful thinking: 'He desired an easier life, wanted
a house to live in, but meanwhile needed the price
of a square meal.'

desiccated

It means dried, not chopped up.

device, devise

A **device** is something designed and made for a specific purpose; to **devise** something is to invent or create something: 'The man who devised the petrol engine gave us a device for propelling a car.'

diagnosis, prognosis

A **diagnosis** is an identification of or an opinion about a problem or disease, while a **prognosis** is a prediction about the outcome.

differ from, differ with

To **differ from** implies a contrast: 'Male views usually differ from those of females.' To **differ with** someone is to disagree.

Who's coming to dinner, supper, lunch or tea?

Depending upon your background, your work pattern and where you live in Britain, these terms can be very confusing. An invitation to **dinner** from strangers could be social dynamite! There are many people who eat **luncheon** around 1pm and their main meal, **dinner** (sometimes called **supper**), at 7–8pm. Others have **dinner** at midday and a main meal called **tea** at about 6pm, with a light **supper** before bedtime. Yet other families may have a **lunch** snack before noon, **dinner** at midday, **tea** at around 4pm and **supper** during the evening. **High tea** is a meal replete with meat or fish served late in the afternoon. And this by no means covers all the confusing gastronomic habits of Britain.

different from, different to

The latter is frowned upon, as is **different than**.
Better to use 'dissimilar to' if you must.

dinghy, dingy

A **dinghy** is a small boat; **dingy** means grimy,
soiled, shabby, and occasionally, gloomy.

disc, disk

The two spellings have been slugging it out for a
couple of centuries, although today we tend to
use **disc** to describe flat circular surfaces, and **disk**
in connection with computers, as with floppy
disk. But the usage is still far from uniform.

discreet, discrete

Discreet means careful, circumspect, prudent.
Discrete means separate, unattached, distinct.

disinterested, uninterested

These are not synonyms. To be **disinterested** is
to be impartial, to be uninvolved. To be
uninterested is to lack interest in something, to
be bored: 'Although he was asked to attend the
meeting as a disinterested party, he was
completely uninterested in the proceedings.'

disorient, disorientate

They both mean the same – to be confused or to
lose your bearings – so why not use the shorter
word?

doubtful, dubious

Doubtful is preferred, unless you wish to suggest
something underhand: 'He was doubtful about
the arrangement, especially with so many dubious
characters involved.'

dual, duel

Dual means consisting of two, or double: a **dual** carriageway, **dual** brakes. A **duel** is a contest or combat between two adversaries.

due to

See **because, since, on account of, due to, owing to**

dwarf, midget, pygmy

A **dwarf** is a human, animal or plant of stunted growth. A **midget** is an extremely small person, while a **pygmy** is generally one of several tribes (including the Pygmy tribe), the members of which are undersized by normal human standards.

each

See **both, each**

eager

See **anxious, eager**

eatable, edible

Both are synonymous, perhaps with the distinction that **eatable** implies something more tasty than **edible**: 'The mushroom, once thought to be poisonous, is edible although bitter.'

effect

See **affect, effect**

effective, effectual, efficacious, efficient

This quartet causes much confusion. **Effective** means an action that produces the intended effect; while **effectual** (subtle, this one) means capable of producing the desired effect. **Efficacious** means having the power to produce the intended effect, while **efficient** means competent: 'He was an efficient judge, effective on the bench, with a style that was effectual in clearing up the backlog of cases; above all, he believed in handing out the sort of sentences that were efficacious.'

egoism, egotism

Egoism is a person's undue preoccupation with his or her self, obsessive self-interest. An **egotistical** person is also unduly self-interested but reveals it to all with excessive boasting and a predominance of 'I' in conversations.

either, any

Either means one or other of two: 'Either take it or leave it'; 'There were two books on the desk and I didn't take either of them.' Any refers to more than two: 'There were four books on the desk and I didn't take any of them.' **Either** and **neither** are both singular: 'Either you or I am lying.' Although correct it looks and sounds awkward, so reconstruct: 'Either you are lying or I am.' Also remember the **either/or** and **neither/nor** rule.

Emergent words

New words are always creeping into the language. Many are useful or necessary, but some are not. Do we really need **proactive**? **Inputting**? **Debrief**? This last word makes little sense. If you devalue something you take away value, but how can you debrief someone, which is to take away information that person has gained, without a complete brainwash? It can't be done. As a grammarian wit observed, debrief makes as much sense as decircumcise.

---

elementary, alimentary, elemental

Elementary means returning to first principles,
rudimentary, introductory; **elemental** describes
something that relates to the primitive forces of
nature. **Alimentary** refers to food and eating;
hence the alimentary canal.

emigrant, immigrant

If John Smith leaves Britain to live in Australia,
he's **emigrating** from Britain and **immigrating** to
Australia, where he becomes an **immigrant** or, as
forgetful Australians have it, a **migrant**.

eminent, imminent

An **eminent** person is somebody of note,
distinguished: 'He was the most eminent doctor
of his time.' **Imminent** means impending,
threatening, about to happen: 'Everyone felt that
war was imminent.' There is also a rare word,
immanent, which means inherent.

empathy, sympathy

Sympathy is generally well understood, and
means a sharing of emotions and a feeling of
fellowship with another; also sometimes
commiseration. **Empathy** is an extension of this
to mean a very close identification with the
thoughts and feelings of another: 'In his portrait,
the artist reveals an unusual empathy with the
sitter.'

enervate, energise

Enervate is often used wrongly; it means to drain
and weaken: 'The succession of hot, humid days
left them irritable and enervated.' **Energise** means
the opposite.

enquire, inquire

Although not a hard and fast rule, **enquire** is used in a questioning sense, while **inquire** and **inquiry** refer to an investigation: 'The reporter enquired how the departmental inquiry was going.'

ensure

See **assure, ensure, insure**

envious, enviable, envy, jealousy

Although one of the seven deadly sins, **envy** can imply a casual longing for something as much as deep hatred and malice towards someone possessing something that one wants. **Enviable** is to be worthy of envy: 'He has got himself an enviable position in a bank.' To be **envious** is to feel or show envy. A near synonym is **covet** which is to lust after the possession of someone or something. **Jealousy** is the expression of personal unease about a situation, often involving rivalry, the transfer of affection or love to another, or a suspected infidelity, and tends to surface as irrational behaviour, resentment and spite.

especially, specially

Especially means in particular, exceptionally, while **specially** means of a special kind, individual, particular: 'That dog is my special friend, especially at feeding times.'

evacuate, vacate

Evacuate means to make empty (the bowels) or to remove from: 'The evacuation from the threatened town went smoothly.' **Vacate** means to give up occupancy.

evade, elude, avoid

Avoid means to shun, to keep away from. **Evade** and **elude** are similar and mean to avoid by cleverness or deception. Knowing the difference between avoidance and evasion is important when paying your tax; one is illegal and one is not.

evaluate

See **appraise, apprise, assess, evaluate**

everyone, every one, everybody

'There were ten apples and every one was rotten'; 'There were ten people in the room and everyone was drunk.' Note that they are both singular. **Everybody** and **everyone** are interchangeable; use according to taste.

evidence, proof, testimony

Testimony is the statement of a witness; **evidence** is information presented to support an argument; **proof** is evidence so factual or convincing as to remove any doubt.

evident

See **apparent, evident**

exasperate

See **aggravate, exasperate**

except, unless

Use **except** to imply an omission and **unless** to make a condition: 'I will work every day except Saturday unless you disagree.'

except

See **accept, except**

expect

See **anticipate, expect, hope**

expeditious, expedient

Expeditious means speedy and efficient, while **expedient** implies an action that is convenient for the purpose: 'It was considered expedient to wind up the firm as expeditiously as possible.'

expertise, skill

Expertise is a posh word for **skill**, although it appears to have acquired a broader meaning, encompassing special skill and knowledge tempered by experience.

facility, faculty

Of the various meanings the one that causes most confusion centres on ability. By **facility** we usually mean the ability to do something with apparent ease: 'She had the charming facility to put people at their ease.' By **faculty** or **faculties** we mean our natural or inherent powers (intelligence, sight, hearing, smell, taste, intuition, etc): 'The task ahead was going to challenge all his faculties to the hilt.'

facsimile

See **replica, copy, facsimile**

faint, feint

Faint means weak, feeble, indistinct; and also to lose consciousness. A **feint** is a feigned or pretended attack intended to mislead.

farther, further

Word police insist that **farther** be used in the context of distance, and **further** when speaking or writing figuratively: 'He guessed that Bristol was much farther from London than Bath, but refused to think further about it.' Nowadays the two forms are interchangeable.

feel

See **believe, feel, think**

few, little, less

It is not unusual for a diet-conscious product to assert that it is **less** fattening, **less** expensive and has **less** calories. Two correct out of three; what is meant is **'fewer** calories'. Use **less** with singular nouns, **fewer** with plural nouns. The same goes for **little**: 'Although I have little spare time, I do have a few minutes to spare now.'

fiancé, fiancée

The first is masculine; the second, with the double ee, is feminine.

fill in, fill out

There's logic here; when you **fill in** something, you insert: 'I filled in the gaps; I filled in the form.' When you **fill out** something you add or complete: 'He filled out John's speech with some spicy anecdotes.'

flagrant, blatant

Flagrant is shocking and outrageous; **blatant** is loud and obvious.

flammable

See **inflammable**

flout, flaunt

Flout means to show contempt or deliberately defy; **flaunt** means to show off boastfully.

forego, forgo

Forego means to go before, to precede; **forgo** means to do without, or to give up something.

formally, formerly

Pronounced the same, spelt differently, and often confused. **Formally** means in a formal, ceremonious or established manner. **Formerly** means in past or earlier times.

fortuitous, fortunate

Something that happens by accident or chance is **fortuitous**; if the result is a happy one, it is also **fortunate**: 'Our meeting in the supermarket was fortuitous, and fortunately she remembered the money she owed me.'

frequently

See **commonly, frequently, generally, usually**

frightened, scared, alarmed, afraid

Afraid has a certain permanence about it: 'He was afraid of crossing roads.' To be **frightened**, **scared** or **alarmed** is more a passing experience. You are also frightened or scared *by* ghosts, not *of* ghosts.

gaol, jail

Both are correct but the former is increasingly regarded as being out of date.

genuine

See **authentic**; see also **replica, copy, facsimile**

genteel, gentle, Gentile

Two of these are well understood: **gentle** means tender and kindly, the opposite to rough, coarse and violent; and a **Gentile** is a non-Jewish person. **Genteel** is trickier; it originally meant well-bred and refined but is now mostly used in a mildly sarcastic way to send up ordinary people who ape middle-class lifestyles.

god, God

The Greeks had **gods**; Christians have **God**, the supreme being, always with a capital G.

gourmand, gourmet, epicure, glutton

Deepest in the trough is the **glutton**, who will eat anything and any amount of it. Then comes the **gourmand**, who, while appreciating what he's eating, loves to eat. Finally, the **gourmet** and the **epicure**, both of whom appreciate the finer points of eating and drinking except that to the **epicure** the joy of food is almost a religion.

guarantee, warranty

Although somewhat interchangeable, a **guarantee** is an agreement to repair or replace, while a **warranty** is a promise that what is being sold is the vendor's, and is serviceable and fit for the use claimed.

guess, suppose, think

To **guess** is to put forward an opinion; to **suppose** is to assume something is true; to **think** is to arrive at a point of view by meditating or remembering.

gynaecologist, obstetrician

A **gynaecologist** specialises in diseases of the urinary and genital organs of women; an **obstetrician** deals with all aspects of childbirth.

had had, had have

There are times when we all get boxed into a corner with the dual **had**: 'If I had had the time, I'd have . . .' Perfectly grammatical but not a pretty sight. Try to avoid it, and avoid totally **had have** and **had of**.

hence, thence, whence

Think of **here**, **there** and **where**: they went **hence** (from here); they advanced **thence** (from there, or that place); **whence** came the new arrival? (from where?).

hereditary, heredity

Hereditary means transmitting or passing by inheritance; **heredity** is the ability of living things to pass qualities from one generation to another. 'He was given a hereditary title; whether his intellect is a product of heredity or environment is anybody's guess.'

Hindi, Hindu

A **Hindu** is a member of the Indian religion of Hinduism; **Hindi** is the language.

hire, rent, lease, let

Modern marketing has introduced a large degree of interchangeability here: you can now **hire**, **rent** or **lease** a car; you can **hire** or **rent** a hall; you can **rent** or **lease** a building, although strictly speaking, **rent** is the money you pay. To **let** a flat means that temporary possession of the property is granted on payment of an agreed **rent**. He who lets is the **lessor**; he who pays the rent is the **lessee**.

hitherto, previously

Hitherto means up to this time, until now; **previously** means until then, prior to: 'Hitherto we have ignored the demands'; 'Previously, the demands were not unreasonable.'

hoard, horde

A **hoard** is a store or an accumulation; **to hoard** is to collect and store. A **horde** is an unruly and often unpredictable crowd of people.

homicide, manslaughter, murder

Homicide is the killing of one person by another. **Murder** is the unlawful killing of another with 'malice aforethought'. **Manslaughter** is the unlawful killing of another but without premeditation, usually under provocation, in the heat of passion, or through negligence.

hope

See **anticipate, expect, hope**

Hopefully

If you are seeking direction on the use of the word **hopefully** you may read this **hopefully**, or **full of hope**, for that is its traditional meaning. But recently a second meaning has intruded into the language: 'Hopefully, the team will play better next time.' Here, the meaning is **'let's hope'** or **'it is hoped'** and it has occasioned many visits from the word police. However its respectability in this sense can be readily defended; it originated from the German **hoffentlich**, meaning **'I hope so'** and travelled with German migrants to the US last century, there to be translated as – **hopefully**. More recently it crossed the Atlantic to Britain where it resides, a misunderstood and mocked orphan, in dire need of friends.

---

hotel, inn, public house, pub, bar

The services of **hotels** should include meals and accommodation; they need not necessarily be licensed to serve alcoholic liquor. **Public houses** or **pubs** are licensed, as are **inns** and **taverns**; they may or may not serve food or offer accommodation, and all the terms are more or less interchangeable. All have **bars**, from which are dispensed intoxicating drinks, but a **bar** can also be an establishment such as a **wine bar** or **gay bar**.

idea, opinion

An **idea** is a concept, a creation; an **opinion** is a view, judgement, assumption, belief.

Idioms

The words and terms in *Word Check* are almost without exception from the orthodox English vocabulary; what are known as idiomatic expressions – **pay through the nose, don't rub it in, take it to heart**, etc – are altogether omitted. In any case most people, perhaps instinctively, have little trouble with their use in their own language. But what does a foreigner, learning English, make of this group of idiomatic add-ons to the word **look?**

look slippery – be quick
look up – refer to
look out – be wary
look down on – scorn
look up to – respect
look daggers – angry stare
look yourself – act normal
look sharp – be alert
look alive – be awake
look see – make an inspection
look over – examine carefully
look for – search
look to – pay attention
look after – care for

---

if, whether

If an alternative is implied, use **whether**: 'Did you notice whether or not he returned the book?'; not 'Did you notice if he returned the book?'

illegible, unreadable

Illegible is usually taken to mean writing that cannot be deciphered because of fading or damage. **Unreadable** is most often used to describe writing that is bad, tedious or boring.

illiterate, ignorant

An **illiterate** person is not necessarily **ignorant** but for some reason has never learned to read or write.

illusion, allusion, delusion

An **illusion** is a deception of the mind or eye; an **allusion** is a passing reference to something, or mention of something; a **delusion** is a false belief.

immigrant

See **emigrant, immigrant**

imminent

See **eminent, imminent**

immoral

See **amoral, immoral**

imply, infer

To **imply** means to express indirectly, to hint or suggest; to **infer** is to deduce: 'I inferred that they had a bad attitude to working, and implied that I wasn't prepared to put up with their behaviour.'

impracticable, impractical

See **practicable, practical**

in, in to, into

In expresses a place, and is static: 'She is in the bathroom.' Into expresses motion and direction: 'She went into the bathroom.' And recognise the sense of purpose in: 'She walked towards the bathroom and went in to powder her nose.'

inapt, inept

Inapt means unsuitable or inappropriate; inept means clumsy, ill-conceived.

incredible, incredulous

Incredible means unbelievable or beyond belief, but is often used wrongly to mean surprising or wonderful. Incredulous describes the inability to believe.

infectious, contagious

Contagious diseases are transmitted by physical contact; infectious diseases are spread by germs in the air or in fluids.

infinite, infinitesimal

Two easily confused opposites. Something infinite is so great it has no limit; infinitesimal is so small as to be negligible: 'It is a mystery why the scientists took such infinite pains to measure such an infinitesimal difference.'

inflammable, flammable

Inflammable means intensely flammable but there is always the danger that, thinking the 'in' prefix means 'not' in this case, some people may assume that inflammable means not flammable. That's why we're seeing more and more flammable and highly flammable labels on products likely to catch fire.

ingenious, ingenuous

An **ingenious** person is clever and inventive; an **ingenuous** person is someone who is open, frank and candid.

initiate

See **begin, commence, initiate, start**

injury

See **accident, injury**

inquire

See **enquire, inquire**

insolvency, bankruptcy

Insolvency happens when a person can't pay his debts when they are due. If he cannot realise his assets he may be declared **bankrupt**, the official, public state of insolvency, when assets are distributed to creditors. When a company goes bust it goes into **liquidation**, either compulsorily or voluntarily.

insurance

See **assurance, insurance**

insure

See **assure, ensure, insure**

invariably, always

Invariably means fixed, unchanged and never varying; **always** means uninterruptedly, at all times. The difference is thus subtle and rarely observed.

irony, sarcasm, satire

You're waiting for a bus, the rain is belting down and you are splashed by passing cars. The next person in the queue says, 'Lovely day, isn't it?' That's **irony**: saying something the opposite of

what you mean with the intention of mocking.
Sarcasm is a bitter, derisory form of irony: 'Well,
thanks for telling everyone about our secret!'
Satire is the witty demolition of stupidity,
wickedness and folly.

It, its, it's

You cannot go through the day without
using **it** a few hundred times. Nor, it seems,
can you go through the day without seeing
its or **it's** used wrongly. The only time **its**
has an apostrophe is when it is used as a
contraction for **it is**: 'It's raining'. The
possessive form of **it** is **its**, always without
an apostrophe: 'The bird fell off its perch.'
When in doubt, read it: 'The bird fell off
it's perch' would sound like, 'The bird fell
off it is perch', which is plainly wrong. So
don't do it.

---

jail
See **gaol, jail**

jealousy
See **envious, enviable, envy, jealous**

Jew
You don't refer to a Christian as a Christian
person or a Hindu as a Hindu person, so why
say 'a Jewish person' or a 'person of the Jewish
persuasion' when you mean a **Jew**?

judicial, judicious
Judicial refers exclusively to justice and the law
courts; **judicious** means showing good judgment,
and also prudent and expedient.

kerb

See **curb, kerb**

kind of, sort of, type of

These are all interchangeable except in the informal sense of 'He sort of has a funny effect on me', and 'I felt kind of relieved it was all over.' The important grammatical point, however, is that **kind**, **sort** and **type** are all singular. 'This kind of TV programme' becomes in the plural 'These kinds of TV programme' and not 'These kinds of TV programmes'.

kipper, herring, bloater

Each of these is the sea fish **herring**. When split, salted and smoked it is called a **kipper**; a **bloater** is a herring cured whole without being split open.

laid, lain, lay, lie

Remember the difference between **lay** and **lie** by reciting: 'Lay down the law and lie on the floor.' In other words, to **lay** is to put or set down something, while to **lie** is to recline. The same goes for **laid** and **lain**: laid is something put down, while **lain** is something or somebody reclining: 'After he laid the table, he went to lie down.' 'The corpse was lying on the floor; it had lain there for days.' **Lay/laying/laid**; **lie/lying/lain**. What may give you grief, though, is **lay** when used as **lie** in the past tense: 'She simply lay there and cried.'

lama, llama

A **lama** is a Tibetan or Mongolian monk; a **llama** is a South American animal.

lawful, legal, legitimate

Lawful means permitted by law; **legal** means relating to law. **Legitimate** has a wider range of meanings – proper, natural, conforming to custom – but often refers to children born in wedlock or legally descended.

Lawyer, barrister, solicitor, silk

A **lawyer** is a member of the legal profession and is usually a barrister or a solicitor. A **barrister** pleads in the courts; a **solicitor** is a legal advisor to his clients and to barristers. An **attorney** is a practitioner in Common Law, while a **notary public** verifies contracts and deeds and administers oaths. A **silk** is a barrister who dons a silk gown on becoming a Queen's Counsel.

---

less

See **few**, **little**, **less**

libel, slander

A **libel** is something written, published or broadcast that damages the character and reputation of someone. **Slander** is spoken defamation.

licence, license

A **licence** (noun) is the piece of paper, evidence of permission granted; **license** (verb) is the act of authorising: 'He was granted a licence to sell liquor and became a licensed victualler.'

lightening, lightning

'As the sky was lightening at dawn, flashes of lightning illuminated the horizon.'

likely, liable, apt

Likely is a useful word to express degrees of probability: 'It is likely to be a fine day today.' **Liable** indicates a strong probability but,

curiously, is almost always used in a negative
sense: 'It is liable to rain today', derived no doubt
from the word's primary meaning of being
exposed to an obligation: 'We could be liable for
damages.' **Apt** implies suitability,
appropriateness or having a tendency to
something: 'At his age he's apt to tire easily.'

literal, literary, literate, literally, littoral

If someone says, 'He literally hammered the guy
into the ground', you should expect to see the
flattened remains of a person merging with the
earth. **Literal** means actual; unfortunately rather
too many of us use it in the opposite sense; what
we really mean is 'figuratively'. **Literate** means
having the ability to read and write, and **literary**
means pertaining to literature. **Littoral** is the odd
man out; it is a shoreline.

loan, lend, lent

Loan is a financial transaction: you can raise a
loan from a bank. However, you can **lend**
someone a book: 'The bank loaned him £5,000';
'She lent me the books last week.'

loose, lose

Use **loose** to describe anything free, hanging,
unfastened: 'She loved loose clothing'; 'The
vampire was on the loose again.' **Lose** describes
loss: 'Give him money and he's sure to lose it.'

lunch

See **dinner, supper, lunch or tea**

maintain

See **claim, allege, assert, maintain**

majority, more, most

More means greater – in quantity, number, extent and importance; so does **most**, except that it implies an estimate. **Majority** also means more, but only of things that can be counted; **minority** is its opposite. The clichés, 'vast majority' and 'tiny minority' are therefore wrong.

malevolent, malicious, malignant

Of this similar trio, **malevolent** is the closest to evil intent; **malicious** implies a premeditated desire to hurt and injure; **malignant** means capable of harm to a life-threatening degree.

manslaughter

See **homicide, manslaughter, murder**

mantel, mantle

Mantel is the shortened form of mantelpiece, while a **mantle** is a cloak or covering.

masterful, masterly

Masterful means imperious, domineering, self-willed. **Masterly** implies extreme skill: 'With a flurry of masterly strokes he finished the painting.'

may

See **can, may, might**

may be, maybe

May and **be** are two words: 'It may be correct'; 'I may be ill tomorrow.' **Maybe** means perhaps or possibly: 'Maybe I'll be ill tomorrow.'

meantime, meanwhile

A lot of interchangeability here, as both can be used as adverbs and nouns: 'In the meantime, I waited in vain'; 'Meanwhile we waited as patiently as we could.'

media, medium

The **media** is the agglomeration of newspapers, magazines, television and radio stations, cable and telephone networks whose business is communications. **Media** is the plural of **medium**; *The Times* is a print medium; the BBC is a broadcast medium.

meretricious, meritorious

The first means superficial and flashy but empty and valueless; the second means excellent and praiseworthy.

Halfway test

Some of the statements below contain words that are used incorrectly. Can you identify them without reference to *Word Check*? Answers over the page.

1. Smoking adversely effected his breathing
2. He depreciated the comedian's efforts to amuse the crowd
3. She did the majority of her washing at the laundry
4. It was fortuitous that we bumped into each other
5. The explosive gas diffused through the city
6. The place was decimated; nobody was left alive
7. The captain was borne aloft by the delighted crowd
8. After an enjoyable shower he felt enlivened and enervated

---

middle

See **centre, middle**

midget

See **dwarf, midget, pygmy**

might

See **can, may, might**

millennium

The second **millennium** is just around the corner so watch the spelling. It's one thousand years.

minimum, minimal, minimize, minuscule

Minimum and **minimal** mean the smallest, the least possible: 'The minimum amount served from this pump is two litres'; 'He was taxed at the minimal rate'. To **minimize** is to reduce to the smallest possible amount, degree, extent or size. **Minuscule** (watch the 'u') means anything extremely small.

Misuse malapropisms

Here are some finely turned malapropisms from writers who should know better:

- The Saxons had coarse mating on the floor.
- In the Middle Ages, ploughs were drawn by bollocks.
- At ancient feasts the head of a bore was put on a platter.
- They found tools, dishes and bowels at the burial site.
- The restaurant will be remembered in the anals of gastronomy.
- The island people were much feared Satin worshippers.

---

moral, morale

Moral concerns right and wrong in human character and conduct; **morale** is a mental state of confidence and optimism: 'The moral standards of the officers had a bad effect on the morale of the troops.'

Answers to Halfway test

Statements 4, 5 and 7 are correct. The incorrect statements should read:
1. Smoking adversely **affected** his breathing. 2. He **deprecated** the comedian's efforts. 3. She did **most** of her washing at the laundry. 6. To **decimate** is to reduce by one in ten, so a better way of expressing the scene would be: 'The place was totally destroyed; nobody was left alive.' 8. After an enjoyable shower he felt enlivened and **energized**.

---

mortgagee, mortgagor

A **mortgagee** borrows the money; a **mortgagor** provides the loan.

Moslem, Muslim

The latter is now the accepted form for a member of the Islamic religion.

murder

See **homicide, manslaughter, murder**

must

The overuse of the word **must**, as in, 'A visit to the British Museum is an absolute must', can be discouraged by remembering that in Anglo-Indian a **must** is the frenzied state of an elephant on heat.

mutual, common

There is a difference. **Common** means something shared by two or more or all; **mutual** implies something shared, experienced or felt between two: 'The boys' reluctance to share the blame was mutual'; 'In the end the various parties found common ground.'

nadir, zenith

The **nadir** is the lowest point of anything; the **zenith** is the highest point.

naturalist, naturist

A **naturalist** studies natural history; a **naturist** enjoys natural surroundings – in the nude.

nauseated, nauseous

If a terrible sight made you feel **nauseated**, you woud describe it as a **nauseous** sight.

necessities, necessaries, essentials

Few people preserve the differences here because they are extremely subtle. In usage, they have all come to mean about the same, which is why we are prone to add prefixes like 'bare necessities' and 'absolute essentials'.

negligent, negligible

To be **negligent** is to be careless and indifferent, to neglect something, often to a dangerous degree. **Negligible** means unimportant, trivial, insignificant.

neither, none, nor

Neither means not either of two, and thus, like **either**, is singular: 'Neither of his two novels is read much nowadays.' And while **either** is followed by **or**, **neither** is followed by **nor**: 'Neither Jane nor Thomas is to go out today.'

None simply means not one; whether it is singular or plural is open to argument and subject to circumstance: 'Not one of my colleagues is supporting me' could be written, 'None of my colleagues are supporting me'.

net, nett

The former is correct.

nevertheless, none the less

Nevertheless means however, yet, notwithstanding. **None the less** (in America written as one word) means 'not any the less': 'I was quite ill; nevertheless I felt I should go'; 'Although I was none the less eager to go, my illness prevented me.'

New York, New York

New York is both a city and a state, hence New York (city), New York (state). To avoid ambiguity, the city is called New York City (NYC). Manhattan is not New York City but one of its five boroughs; the others are Bronx, Brooklyn, Queens and Staten Island.

nice

Of the two meanings, only that of 'discriminating and precise' retains its original definition; the second meaning – variously agreeable, pleasant, attractive, kind – has through overuse attracted an entire layer of vague meanings. Replace by more specific adjectives to convey what you really mean.

noisome, noisy

Noisy needs no explanation, but noisome has nothing to do with noise: it means objectionable and offensive.

no one, no-one

No one is at home means that nobody, no person, not anyone is at home. It is written as two words for obvious reasons (noone!) although some prefer to hyphenate.

notable, noted, notorious

If you are notable you are a person distinguished by some aspect of worthiness or character. If you are noted it is usually because of some outstanding skill or achievement: 'He was a noted bassoon player.' If you are notorious you are a celebrity for all the wrong reasons.

noxious, obnoxious

See obnoxious, noxious

nutritious, nutritional

Certain foods may be nutritious, meaning nourishing, but not nutritional, which refers to the process of nourishing the body: 'The nutritional needs of the patients require at least two nutritious meals a day.'

objective, subjective

To be objective means to be uninfluenced by any prior beliefs, personal feelings or prejudices. To be subjective is to be the opposite, to be over-influenced by personal considerations or relationships.

obligate, oblige

Of the two, **obligate** implies a moral or legal duty, while **oblige** means to render a favour or to accommodate: 'The man had obliged him on several occasions, and now he felt obligated to repay the loan.'

obnoxious, noxious

Obnoxious is usually applied to personal behaviour and means aggressively unpleasant. **Noxious** is something potentially injurious.

obsolete, obsolescent

If something is **obsolete** it is out of use or out of date; if it is **obsolescent** it is in the process of becoming obsolete.

obstetrician

See **gynaecologist, obstetrician**

obviate, obliterate

Obviate means to remove, to make unnecessary: 'The new car park will obviate the need for people to park in the street.' **Obliterate** means to remove or efface by destruction.

odious, odorous

Odious means unpleasant and detestable; **odorous** applies only to smells, and may be pleasant. To describe a bad smell, use **malodorous**.

official, officious

Official implies the holding of a position of authority; **officious** means self-important and unnecessarily intrusive: 'The official in charge was officious in the extreme.'

off of

'He told us to get off of the grass' is wrong. Lose the **of**: 'He told us to get off the grass.'

one, one's, oneself

The use of **one** ('One isn't obliged to use the indefinite pronoun but it can be useful at times') can often lead to inelegancy and pompousness as any sentence containing it must use **one's** and **oneself**: 'No matter how much one tries to protect one's life, in a war it is only too easy to hurt oneself.' Many good writers go through life without ever using this form, preferring the more idiomatic: 'No matter how much you try to protect your life, you can still get hurt in a war.'

ongoing, continuing

Ongoing is an 'in-word' (ongoing dialogue/ situation/programme) for which there are better choices: **continuing, developing**, etc.

on to, onto

Until recently, **on to** as a single word was unrecognised. Both forms are interchangeable, except in the sense of: 'He refuelled, then drove the car on to his destination.'

opponent

See **adversary, opponent**

opportunity, chance, possibility

Chance, as any gambler knows, is a force by which things happen without cause; **opportunity** is the recognition of a favourable opening; **possibility** is the likelihood of something happening or existing.

Optical options

Ophthalmologists and **oculists** are medical
doctors who specialise in diseases of the eye.
An **optometrist** tests eyes and vision and
prescribes, while an **optician** fills out
prescriptions and makes and sells spectacles.
Artificial eyes are made by **ocularists**.

or, nor

See **neither, none, nor**

oral, aural, verbal

Oral refers to the mouth, thus spoken; **aural**
refers to the ear, thus heard. **Verbal** refers to
words, spoken or written, and can be ambiguous
if not used correctly. An **oral** examination is one
that is spoken. A **verbal** agreement may or may
not be in writing; if the former, specify 'written
agreement'.

ordinary

See **average, ordinary**

orient, orientate

As with **disorient** and **disorientate**, they are
interchangeable.

orthopaedic, paediatric

An **orthopaedist** was once the medical specialist
who treated deformities in children, and this is
why there is confusion between the two terms.
Nowadays an **orthopaedist** treats the bone, joint
and muscle problems of children and adults; a
paediatrician treats children only.

overly

The use of this word is common enough ('She was not overly fond of cabbage') but continues to be frowned upon. Purists might suggest: 'She was not over-enthusiastic about cabbage.'

paediatric

See **orthopaedic, paediatric**

pair

See **couple, pair**

palate, palette, pallet

The **palate** is the roof of the mouth; a **palette** is an artist's board on which colours are mixed; a **pallet** is many things but most visibly the robust timber tray on which are stacked bulky goods for easy lifting and transportation.

parameter, perimeter

A **perimeter** is a boundary or limit. A **parameter**, a very much misused jargon word, is a mathematical term for a constant, with variable values, used to determine a problem – nothing to do with boundaries at all.

part from, part with

To **part from** someone means to leave; to **part with** something is to give it away or give it up.

partial, partially, partly

Partial can mean either prejudiced, or incomplete, so only use it when the meaning is clear: a 'partial account' of some event could mean either. The same applies to **partially**, so if in doubt, use **partly**.

Passable pairs

Quite a few words in the language have evolved with two spellings, both of which are acceptable. Here are some examples:

gipsy, gypsy	leaped, leapt
hoofs, hooves	learned, learnt
movable, moveable	leaned, leant
hiccup, hiccough	racism, racialism
instal, install	spelled, spelt

passed, past

'We saw the car pass at tremendous speed'; 'We told the police that the car passed at a great speed'; 'But that was ages ago; it was in the past.'

per, a

'We worked ten hours per day' is considered inferior to the plain 'We worked ten hours a day.' Restrict the use of **per** to commercial or legal contexts, as in 'per annum'.

perceptible, perceptive, percipient

Perceptible means observable or able to be recognised or measured. **Perceptive** means 'quick to see and understand'; **percipient** is a near synonym, except that in this case the perceiving has a hint of the unexplainable about it.

peremptory, perfunctory

Peremptory means final, decisive, precluding questions and objections. **Perfunctory** means careless and half-hearted: 'After drilling in such a perfunctory manner, the squad was peremptorily ordered to the cookhouse.'

63

permanent, perennial

Perennial does not, as many people seem to believe, mean 'year after year'; its correct meaning is **permanent**, unfailing, unceasing, long-lived.

perpetrate, perpetuate

Perpetrate means to commit something, to carry something out; **perpetuate** means to preserve by making eternal: 'He perpetrated such a wonderful hoax that the event was perpetuated by an annual dinner.'

perquisite, prerequisite

Easily confused. A **perquisite** (perk) is a benefit or privilege, often regarded as a right; a **prerequisite** is a precondition: 'One of the men's prerequisites for a settlement was not to take away the car parking perquisite.'

personal, personnel

Personal is an adjective ('I've been going through my personal expenses') while **personnel** is a noun meaning the staff of a company or organisation.

perspicacity, perspicuity

The first means 'clearness of understanding'; the second, 'clearness of statement'. As Eric Partridge put it: 'Perspicacity is needed to grasp the distinction, and perspicuity to explain it.'

persuade

See **convince, persuade**

peruse, read

Peruse is often believed to mean reading something casually, at a glance. It means the opposite, which is to read and examine carefully and critically.

petition, partition

A **petition** is a request, a plea, a formal written supplication to some authority; a **partition** is a dividing wall.

Petrol and other hydrocarbons

Petroleum is what comes out of the oil well, and **petrol** (**gasoline** or **gas** in the US) is refined from it. **Paraffin** (**kerosine** in the US, Australia and other countries) is also distilled from petroleum. What comes out of the pumps marked **derv** (Diesel Engined Road Vehicle) is **diesel** oil, one of the heavier fractions broken down from the crude petroleum.

---

plaid

See **tartan, plaid**

podium

See **dais, lectern, podium, rostrum**

possible, plausible, feasible

Possible means that something can exist, happen, or be done; **feasible** means that something is capable of being done. If an argument or statement appears to be reasonable or true it is **plausible**: 'The plan was plausible, for although the river was subject to flooding it was still feasible to construct the bridge.'

practicable, practical

Practicable means feasible, capable of being done and put into practice. **Practical** has a wider range of meanings, including useful, usable, sensible, realistic, efficient: 'It was practicable to climb the wall with a rope, but a more practical plan was to get a ladder.' Their opposites, **impracticable**

and **impractical**, mean 'unfeasible, impossible, unattainable' and 'useless, ineffective' respectively.

practically, virtually

These often confused words have quite different meanings. **Practically** means in practice, effectively, while **virtually** means almost, very nearly: 'Living on anything they could find, the people were practically starving, and clean water was virtually non-existent.'

practice, practise

'The doctor had **practised** medicine for nearly forty years, thirty of them from his **practice** in Harley Street.'

precede, proceed, supersede

To **precede** is to go before or come before; to **proceed** is to continue or to go forward: 'As they proceeded to the altar, the Archbishop **preceded** the Queen.' **Supersede** means to displace or replace someone or something: 'Many people regretted that the Authorised Version had been superseded by the Revised English Bible.'

predicate, predict

Predicate seems to be catching on as a synonym for **predict**, which it is not. **Predict** means to foretell, while the original meaning of **predicate** is to imply, affirm or assert: 'He predicated that the election result would turn on the issue of inflation but declined to predict the result.' In the US, **predicate** almost always means **based**: 'His views on economic policy are predicated on the need to lower inflation.'

pre-empt, prevent

To **pre-empt** is to do something or obtain something beforehand, to appropriate something in advance of other claims. To **prevent** is to hinder or stop.

premier, première

Premier means first or foremost and is often used as a title for a country's leading statesman. **Première** is used exclusively for first performances of plays and films: 'After its **première** in London next week the play will **première** in New York in August.'

prescribe, proscribe

The words are opposites: **prescribe** means to recommend a course of action or lay down rules, while **proscribe** means to banish or forbid: 'Smoking is proscribed on the Underground.'

presume

See **assume, presume**

preventative, preventive

Both mean 'to prevent something from happening or recurring', but a fine difference is emerging. **Preventative** is used as a noun: 'Against the common cold, vitamin C is an effective preventative; that's the view of preventive medicine.'

previously

See **hitherto, previously**

principal, principle

A very tricky duo. The meanings of **principle** are fairly straightforward: a fundamental truth, a belief or doctrine, an agreed rule of action or conduct. **Principal** can be an adjective (meaning of chief importance) or a noun (meaning the leader, the head; or a sum of money on which interest accrues): 'The school principal said his principal aim was to insist on students observing a code of strict moral principles.'

Of proctors and prostates

A not uncommon malapropism goes something like this: 'He's seeing the doctor because of his prostrate trouble.' **Prostrate** means to lie face down, while the **prostate** is a male reproductive gland that tends to peter out with age. And a **proctor**, perhaps because it rhymes with doctor, is sometimes thought to specialise in diseases of the anus. In fact a **proctologist** does that; a **proctor** is a university official, one of two elected annually.

---

prognosis
See **diagnosis, prognosis**

program, programme
Programme (program in the US) is still preferred in Britain, although **program** has made considerable inroads in the computer industry.

prone, prostrate, recumbent, supine
The good news is that they all refer to lying down. The bad news is that they all have different meanings. To lie **prone** is to lie face downwards; **prostrate** assumes the same position but suggests exhaustion and helplessness. **Recumbent** is lying in any comfortable position, while **supine** is lying listlessly on the back, looking upwards.

proposal, proposition
While both mean 'something suggested', **proposal** is more of an offer, as in a **proposal** of marriage; a **proposition** is a stronger suggestion, even an assertion, that might invite discussion

before agreement. That said, they are both fairly
interchangeable.

Psycho matters

This is an area of potentially embarrassing
confusion. **Psychosis** is the generic term for
disorders of the mind marked by a loss of
touch with reality; **psychotics** suffer from
psychoses, and **psychiatry** is the branch of
medical science which deals with mental
disorders and their diagnosis, treatment and
prevention. **Psychotics** may be
psychopaths, persons with anti-social
personality disorders; **schizophrenics**,
whose minds and feelings have parted,
causing a withdrawal from reality; or
neurotics, persons with unbalanced minds
suffering from obsessive behaviour,
unreasonable fears and hysteria. **Psychology**
is the study of the mind and its behaviour;
psychoanalysis is a treatment method based
on the patient's memory of his or her past
life; **psychotherapy** is a treatment based on
action on the mind itself and not on the use
of drugs or operations.

---

purposely, purposefully

Purposely means on purpose, intentionally.
Purposefully means the same but with added
determination, and with some definite purpose or
objective in mind.

quantitative, qualitative

Quantitative refers to quantity and proportions,
of amounts, size and volume; **qualitative** refers
to quality, of characteristics, properties, attributes
and singularities.

quantity, number

Use **number** only when the total can be counted: 'To make the juice you use a large number of oranges and a large quantity of water.'

quantum leap

This term is used rather loosely; strictly speaking it is a change or an advance of unprecedented magnitude with no apparent connection with anything that preceded it.

quite, rather

Because the meaning of **quite** is completely, entirely, absolutely ('He flung himself down, quite exhausted') it seems odd that we persist in using it to mean **somewhat**, **sort of** and **rather**: 'The horse was going quite well until the fifth jump.' **Rather** is preferred.

quorum, quota

A **quorum** is the agreed number of people required to be present before a meeting can be held; a **quota** is a proportion, a limit, an agreed number or amount.

rain, reign, rein

Rain we all know about; **to reign** is to rule and a **reign** is a period during which a particular monarch rules; to **rein** is to check or control, and a **rein** is the strap which controls and guides a horse: 'The constant rain of criticism did nothing to stop Henry VIII giving full rein to his appetites throughout his entire reign.'

raise, raze, rise

To **raise** is to elevate; to **raze** is to do the reverse: to destroy completely, to level with the earth. **Raise** is also creeping in to mean 'rear children', but most people would prefer to **raise** sheep and

bring up a family. You also **raise** your head but
rise in the morning and **rise** from your chair.
British English still prefers a **pay rise** to the
American **raise**.

rapt, wrapped

Rapt means engrossed and absorbed; **wrapped**
means enveloped, enfolded, blanketed.

react, respond

A **reaction** is a **response** to some stimulus, so
react is an extremely vague term. To be more
precise, use words like **respond** and **reply**. 'His
immediate response was to reply in no uncertain
terms.'

really

See **actually, virtually, really**

rebut, refute, repudiate, deny

There are several shades of meaning among this
lot. To **rebut** is to contradict by argument; to **deny**
is to assert that an allegation or statement is false;
to **repudiate** is to disown, reject or refuse to
admit a charge or claim; and to **refute** – the
strongest and most convincing denial of all – is
to prove that an accusation is false.

receipt, recipe

A **receipt** is a written acknowledgement that
something has been received; a **recipe** is a
formula of ingredients and instructions to make
something, usually in cookery. However, in the
past, receipt meant the same as recipe.

recoup, recover

Recoup means to regain or replace a loss, usually
financial; **recover** is used in a broader way:
'When he recovered from the fainting spell he
also recovered his composure.'

reduce, lessen

Virtually interchangeable, except that **lessen** tends to be used where numbers are involved in the quantity: 'By reducing his petrol consumption, he lessened the number of weekly trips to the garage.'

regretful, regretfully, regrettable, regrettably

The first two mean to feel sorry or show regret, while the second pair is used when sorrow or regret is caused: 'Regretfully, I am forced to cancel our plans'; 'The problems caused by the cancellation are regrettable, but I had no other option.'

regulate, relegate

Regulate means to adjust, control or restrict; **relegate**, as any football fan knows, means to consign to an inferior position.

reiterate, repeat

Repeat is to do, make or say something again. If there is a difference it is that **reiterate** tends to be used to express the repetition of a word, statement, account or request often in order to stress it.

relatively, comparatively

Use only when there is something to be relative to, or something to compare with: 'Although it appeared to be a most ambitious project, it would occupy relatively/comparatively little of his time.'

replica, copy, facsimile

It is generally accepted that a **replica** is a duplicate made by the original artist, or made under his supervision. A **facsimile** is a copy exact in every respect and detail. A **copy** is the most general term and can be a duplicate (a Xerox) or state-of-the-art colour reproduction, or anything in between.

replicate, repeat

Although increasingly used as a synonym for **repeat**, **replicate** means rather more than that. Technically, a **replication** is a repeat of a study or of research, using the same data and methods, to confirm whether the result will be the same.

repudiate

See **rebut, refute, repudiate, deny**

respectably, respectfully, respectively

Respectably means in a way that is honest, decent and deserving respect. **Respectfully** means with respect. **Respectively** means in the order given: 'John, Amy and Sarah are aged twelve, nine and five respectively.'

restful, restive, restless

Restive and **restless** are the opposite to **restful**, which means peaceful, calm, inviting rest. A **restless** person is one who cannot be still or quiet, while a **restive** person (although more often a horse) is one who frets under restraint.

restaurant, restaurateur

The latter owns or manages the former; note the spelling.

revenge, avenge

Revenge is personal retaliation: 'I eventually got my revenge by having him arrested for harassment.' To **avenge** a wrong, the punishment is meted out by a third party as a form of rough justice: 'They avenged my father's murder.'

reverse
See **converse, inverse, obverse, reverse**

review, revue
'The revue had been enthusiastically received but the cast was shattered by the savage review in *Variety*.'

rheumatism, arthritis
Rheumatism is a term covering a variety of painful diseases of the joints and muscles; **arthritis** is local inflammation of a particular joint.

robbery
See **burglary, robbery, stealing, theft**

Roman Catholic
See **catholic, Catholic**

rostrum
See **dais, lectern, podium, rostrum**

saccharin, saccharine
The first is the sugar substitute; the second means excessively sweet.

sacred, sacrosanct
Sacred means dedicated to religious use: holy, and not to be profaned. **Sacrosanct** is more intensive, and means 'incapable of being violated, pure and incorruptible'.

sadism, masochism
Sadism is the desire to inflict physical pain on others and derive pleasure [usually sexual] from it; **masochism** is the desire to be physically abused or humiliated by another [usually for sexual pleasure].

salary, wages, remuneration

A **salary** is usually fixed as an annual rate, and divided into months or weeks; **wages** are rates paid by the day or week. **Remuneration** is payment for a service, not necessarily on a regular basis.

same, similar

'Harry sold six cars last week, and a similar number this week.' What is meant here is 'the same number this week'; **similar** means resembling something or someone.

sanatorium, sanitarium

The first offers curative services, as with health farms and rest homes; the second is a little-used term for a hospital.

sarcasm, satire

See **irony, sarcasm, satire**

sceptical

See **cynical, sceptical**

Scotland, Scotsman, Scot and Scotch

Natives and institutions of Scotland are Scottish or Scots: Scotswoman, Scottish smoked trout, Scottish writers. There are a few exceptions including Scotch broth and, of course, Scotch whisky (not whiskey, that's made in Ireland).

---

see, witness

To **see** is to observe something with your eyes; to **witness** something is to observe with the eyes and other senses: 'I saw the car go past but did not witness the accident.'

sensitive, sensual, sensuous

Sensitive means acutely susceptible to influences, highly responsive to stimulus, easily offended. A near synonym is **sensibility**, but this has come to mean heightened feelings for what is socially correct. **Sensual** pleasure derives from physical indulgences like eating, drinking and sex; **sensuous** refers to arousal through all the senses: listening to music, smelling a flower, watching a sunset, feeling silk, etc.

sewage, sewerage

Perhaps you may need to know this one day: **sewerage** is the sewer system, and **sewage** is what passes through it.

shall, will

Full directions for the correct use of **shall** and **will** would frighten most people, so it's not surprising that the distinctions have largely disappeared, helped on their way by the increasing adoption of the contractions **I'll**, **she'll**, **he'll**, **they'll**, which can mean either. Churchill further hastened the rot with his 'We shall fight on the beaches . . .' speech, in which he consistently used **shall** instead of **will** in the first person to express determination. Writers and speakers wishing to preserve traditional usage are advised to consult any good grammar book. Meanwhile, the use of **shall** is now almost confined to 'officialese': 'Passengers shall not talk to the driver while the vehicle is in motion.'

should, would

The fate of **shall** has also befallen **should** because of an overdose of complex rules. 'I should like to see some of your work' looks and sounds elegant but in modern usage it has largely been replaced by **would** or **I'd**.

silicon, silicone

Silicon is the chemical element which is all about us in the form of sand; **silicone** is a synthetic silicon compound used to make lubricants, water repellants and a range of other products.

simile, metaphor

A **simile** uses a direct comparison, usually preceded by as, as if, or like: 'He was as thick as two planks'; 'The party went like a house on fire.' A **metaphor** makes an analogy: 'You're a doll'; 'She's a pain in the neck.' A **mixed metaphor** combines two incompatible metaphors: 'We've got a real headache on our hands'; 'This decision is a very hard blow to swallow.'

It's a problem situation

A **situation** is, simply, a position or location, or a state of affairs. Yet the word is being increasingly used superfluously ('crisis situation' to mean crisis; 'emergency situation' to mean emergency) and ambiguously (a mother–daughter situation – meaning what?). Be wary.

---

slander

See **libel, slander**

sleight, slight

Sleight means dexterity, as in the 'sleight of hand' of a magician; **slight** means small, slim, insignificant.

so-called

This is regarded as a put-down or sneer term, like **self-styled, would-be** and **self-proclaimed**. It indicates that what follows is to be held up to question or ridicule: 'The so-called animal lovers said they had collected a petition of ten thousand names.'

solecism, solipsism

In linguistic terms, a **solecism** is a violation of conventional usage, more or less confined to faulty syntax and incorrect pronunciation. **Solipsism** is the theory that only the self is real and knowable.

sort of

See **kind of, sort of**

source, cause

The difference is illustrated by: 'The source of his headache was that blow to his head.' In fact, the blow was the **cause**; the **source** may have been a punch by a boxer, a thrown brick or running into a wall.

specially

See **especially, specially**

specialty, speciality

The first is preferred in the US, but both are interchangeable.

stationary, stationery

Stationary means fixed, not moving, standing still; stationers sell writing material, which is called **stationery**.

straightened, straitened

You **straighten** something by making or bending it straight; **straitened** means restricted: 'The couple lived in straitened circumstances.'

strategy, tactics, stratagem

Strategy is the planning of an operation, while **tactics** involve putting the strategy into effect. A **stratagem** is a scheme designed to deceive.

Stroke, coronary, heart failure

A **stroke** is a cerebral haemorrhage, a burst blood vessel in the brain that often results in paralysis. A **coronary**, or more correctly a **coronary thrombosis**, is caused by a clot in the coronary artery, stopping the supply of blood to the heart. **Heart failure** or **heart attack** covers a variety of disorders in which the heart is suddenly unable to cope with pumping blood to the body. Most heart failures are treatable.

---

subconscious, unconscious

Subconscious has two meanings: that of being only partly aware, and, more commonly, the thoughts that occupy the hidden level of the mind and influence our actions. To be **unconscious** is to be unaware: 'She was unconscious of the danger she was in.' It can also mean total loss of consciousness: 'After the accident he was unconscious for two days.'

subjective

See **objective, subjective**

substitute, replace

A subtle but interesting difference: **substitute** means to 'put in the place of', while **replace** means to 'put back again in place': 'She carefully replaced the candlesticks but substituted a cheap imitation for the priceless bowl.'

successive

See **consecutive, successive**

supersede

See **precede, proceed, supersede**

suppose

See **guess, suppose, think**

surely, certainly, definitely

Certainly and **definitely** are interchangeable and so, for the most part, is **surely**. However **surely** can also imply safely and securely: 'He made his way slowly but surely up the cliff face', and is also used to emphasise a question: 'Surely you're not going to climb up there?'

swingeing, swinging

Swingeing (pronounced swinjing) means severe in degree: 'People tend to forget that the Swinging Sixties also saw swingeing tax increases.'

sympathy

See **empathy, sympathy**

synthesis

See **analysis, synthesis**

tactics

See **strategy, tactics, stratagem**

Tales from the clypt

As long as there are words that look and sound alike, the merry list of malapropisms will run forever:

- Mrs Connor's doctor was arrested for possession of heroine.
- One of the restaurant's specialties was barely soup.
- He was so angry we thought he'd blow a casket.
- We wrecked our brains trying to think of the answer.
- Most Chinese speak the mandolin dialect.
- I never did like that cold slaw.

tartan, plaid

Tartan is the distinctive patterned cloth used for certain Scottish garments, including the kilt and the **plaid** – the shawl worn over the shoulder.

tasteful, tasty

Tasteful is something that embodies or employs aesthetic discrimination or good taste: 'The reception rooms were tastefully furnished.' **Tasty** means flavourful to the palate, although colloquially it has also come to mean sexually attractive.

testament, testimony

A **testament** is a will, the document by which a person disposes of his estate after death. **Testimony** is evidence, proof or confirmation, often given under oath. See also: **evidence, proof, testimony**

theft

See **burglary, robbery, theft**

That, which, who

That and which are relative pronouns that are becoming more and more interchangeable despite the rules about their use. However, a couple of these rules should be observed. **That** is used to refer to persons, animals and things; **which** to animals and things; **who** and **whom** to persons. Use **that** to restrict or define the meaning or intention of the preceding word or phrase: 'The hotel that Helen stayed at has burnt down.' **That** defines or identifies the hotel for us. Use **which** when the identifying information is already supplied in the sentence: 'The Imperial Hotel at Bath, which Helen stayed at last year, has burnt down.' Whether to use **who** or **that** for persons can be a problem, but generally, **that** is used to refer to any person, and **who** to a particular person: 'The mechanic that fixed this car ought to be shot'; 'My mate Jim, who was supposed to fix the car, ought to be shot.' Most people now solve this problem by using **who** indiscriminately.

their, there, they're

They look different but sound the same and often confuse. **Their** is a possessive pronoun: 'It is their car.' **There** means in or at that place: 'She left the car there; now it's gone.' **They're** is a contraction of 'they are'.

think

See **guess, suppose, think**

though

See **although, though**

till, until

Till is a short form of until, meaning 'up to the time when': 'I'll stay until the bar closes.' Both are interchangeable, but **until** is preferred.

titillate, titivate

The first means to tickle or excite; the second means to smarten up.

TNT, dynamite, gelignite

Dynamite, a compound of liquid nitroglycerin and absorbent material, was the invention of Alfred Nobel in 1866; he followed this with blasting gelatin or **gelignite** in 1875. **TNT** or tri-nitro-toluene is the most recent of the trio and safest from friction and shock.

---

ton, tonne

An English **ton** is 2,240 lbs; a short or American **ton** is 2,000 lbs; a metric **tonne** is 1,000 kilograms or about 2,200 lbs.

tortuous, torturous

Tortuous means twisting, winding, devious; **torturous** means inflicting torture and pain: 'Following the dark, tortuous passages became a torturous nightmare.'

toward, towards

Both, meaning 'in the direction of' or 'in respect of', are interchangeable. Use according to taste, appearance and sound: 'They steered toward/ towards the horizon'; 'The storm broke towards dawn.'

truth

See **veracity, truth**

try and, try to

Try to is correct, and in most cases, sounds better to the ear. Although **try and** is so common as to be considered colloquial, **try to** avoid it.

turbid, turgid

Turbid means clouded, muddy, opaque; **turgid** means swollen, bloated, inflated. A river in flood can be both turgid and turbid.

unaware, unawares

Two different words, two meanings. If you are **unaware** (adjective) you are not aware or you are ignorant of something; if you are caught **unawares** (adverb), something has happened without warning and you are surprised.

unconscious

See **subconscious, unconscious**

under

See **beneath, under**

uninterested

See **disinterested, uninterested**

unique

Unique means without like or equal, the only one of its kind. Yet we persist in using pointless modifiers like 'so unique', 'absolutely unique', 'most unique' and so forth. If you think something may be **unique**, don't say 'nearly unique' but, 'It is so rare, so exceptional, that I think it may be unique.'

unless

See **except, unless**

unprecedented

The free use of this word, which means first, original, unparalleled, unheard-of, can land you into trouble. Announce something or some event as **unprecedented** and the chances are that they are not; further, someone is likely to pop up and smugly point out your error. Make sure of your facts before using it.

unreadable

See **illegible, unreadable**

until

See **till, until**

upon, on

With a couple of exceptions, **upon** and **on** are interchangeable: 'She sat upon/on the chair.' However, you would hardly begin a fairy story with, 'Once on a time . . .'; nor does the ear respond favourably to, 'The suburbs stretched mile on mile . . .'

urban, urbane

Urban refers to the city, as in urban living, urban architecture; **urbane** means poised and sophisticated: 'Ten years of urban life had transformed the country boy into a witty, urbane gentleman.'

use, utilise, usage

Use is synonymous with the other two words in most cases and should be preferred. **Utilise** has the narrow meaning of making useful, or turning to profitable account: 'The company utilised the old factory to manufacture office furniture.'
Usage – especially in the context of the English

language – is the recognised practice of something; it is also applied where quantities are involved: 'Water usage in Kent rose 30% last month.'

valuable, invaluable, valued

Valuable means having great value, or being worth a lot of money. **Invaluable** means priceless, precious beyond valuation: 'Her friendship at this difficult time was invaluable to him.' Apart from its use as 'I'm having my watch valued', meaning to estimate the worth of something, **valued** means esteemed and highly regarded: 'Of all the things he valued most, her friendship was paramount.'

veracity, truth

Truth is something that is true, that is fact. **Veracity** is the capacity for being truthful, accurate and honest: 'We can depend upon his admirable veracity for the truth to come out.'

verbal

See **oral, aural, verbal**

viable, workable

The true meaning of **viable** is 'the capability to maintain independent existence in life'. It has, however, become an overworked and inaccurately used buzz-word, to the extent that a doctor once claimed: 'Suicide is a viable alternative to painful terminal illness.' Try to limit its use to mean capable of surviving and thriving independently: 'The Channel Tunnel is expected to be operationally viable by the year 2010.' **Workable** means something or some plan that is practicable and can be made to work. (See **practicable, practical**; also **possible, plausible, feasible**)

Vicars and other men of God

The differences between **parsons**, **rectors** and **vicars** are largely historic. **Parsons** and **rectors** were the most fortunate because their parochial posts (called a living) included church property and income (called the benefice) and revenue from the parish (called the tithe). The poor **vicar** got none of this, nor did the **curate**, who was an assistant to the parish priest. Their respective residences are called the **parsonage**, **rectory** and **vicarage**. A **curacy** is a position, not a residence.

vicious, viscous

Vicious implies a propensity for vice, hatred, spite and desire to hurt; **viscous** means thick and sticky, and is usually applied to liquids.

virtually

See **practically, virtually**

wages

See **salary, wages, remuneration**

waive, wave

These two are often confused. **Waive** means to relinquish, not to insist on something: 'He waived his right to speak.'

want

See **desire, want, need**

whatever, whatsoever

Whatever means 'no matter what' ('Whatever the problems, I promise to finish the job') and also 'what' ('Whatever is the matter?'). **Whatsoever** is

vaguely synonymous in the context of 'at all':
'Have you no manners whatsoever?' But the usage
that has grown into a monster has resulted from
the hijacking of **whatever** to mean 'and so on and
so forth and who cares anyway?': 'On Saturdays
I usually do some shopping, wash my hair, empty
the cat litter, generally slob around and, you
know, whatever . . .'

whether
See **if**, **whether**

To whomever it may concern: who and whom

Without getting into personal, relative and
predicate pronouns and objects of finite
verbs, it is not easy to explain the rules
governing the use of **who** and **whom**. As a
consequence, popular usage all but
abandons **whom** on the grounds of (a) the
likelihood of using it incorrectly, and (b) it
sounds pompous. Furthermore, exclusive
users of **who** are probably right 80% of the
time. But if you wish to take a stab at
whom, the rough-and-ready **who/whom** –
he/him – **she/her** formula will help: simply
substitute **he** or **she** for **who**, and **him** or
her for **whom**. Thus 'He is a man who/
whom I know is honest.' He is honest? Him
is honest? The answer is he, and therefore
the correct choice is **who**. You can
remember this with the celebrated
Hemingway mnemonic. Which sounds
right: 'For Whom The Bell Tolls? It tolls
for him'; or 'For Who The Bell Tolls? It
tolls for he'?

which
See **that, which, who**

will
See **shall, will**

witness
See **see, witness**

workable
See **viable, workable**

would
See **should, would**

wrapped
See **rapt, wrapped**

Xerox
Many of us say, 'Can you Xerox this for me, please?', even though the copier might be a Canon or some other make. Like Hoover, Durex and Cellophane, Xerox is a trade name, not a generic name, and should be capitalised.

your, yours, you're
Your means belonging to you: 'I love your house'; 'Is that your opinion?' **Yours** denotes the particular one belonging to you: 'Is that jacket yours?'; 'That son of yours is a real tearaway.' It is never spelt with an apostrophe. **You're** is often confused with **your** but it is a contraction of **you are**; thus the contraction of 'You are quite mad!' is 'You're quite mad!'

Yours sincerely, Yours truly
Yours does not have an apostrophe; if it did it would mean 'your is'. **Yours Truly** and **Yours Faithfully** are customarily reserved for impersonal

letters; **Yours Sincerely** when the addressee is named.

zenith

See **nadir, zenith**

Further Reading

Of necessity, *Word Check* confines its listing to distinguishing between the words and expressions most likely to be misused in everyday speech and writing. For more extensive listings of meanings and differences, the following books are recommended:

Dictionary of Difficult Words, Hutchinson, 1992
Confusable Words, Collins, 1992
Good Word Guide, Edited by Martin Manser, Bloomsbury, 1990
Plain English, by Philip Davies Roberts, Penguin, 1988
Room's Dictionary of Differences, Routledge & Kegan Paul, 1981

Good Grammar in One Hour

We all know more about grammar than we think. Yet even the most learned authorities can't claim to know it all. Written with the minimum of jargon, *Good Grammar in One Hour* will allow you to polish your native know-how, and to renew acquaintance with the language and its working.

Crisp, Clear Writing in One Hour

Here are jargon and officialese hammered flat, circumlocution and tautology brutally eliminated, vogue words and verbiage sent packing. In just one hour, a veteran Fleet Street sub-editor steers you away from cliche, euphemism and muddle to leave you with crisp, cogent, pared-down prose of which you can be proud.

Spell Check
1000 Most Misspelled Words

This book deals with slippery orthographic howlers
– like mispelled for misspelled, or sacrilegious,
fuchsia, inoculate, obbligato, and 995 others. *Spell
Check* will guide you through the most deceptive,
puzzling and troublesome words, including proper
nouns such as Sikh, Sarajevo, Beaulieu and
Reykjavik, and exceptions to rules such as '*i* before
e except after *c*'.

Word Bank
Expanding Your Vocabulary

The better you are at communicating, the more
successful you are likely to be – and an effective
vocabulary is the guarantee of clear, assured and
persuasive speech and writing. *Word Bank* will
expand your vocabulary and add force to your
reasoning, conversation and self-confidence.

The Name Book

What's in a name? Here is everything you ever needed to know about surnames, Christian names, nicknames and odd names: what they mean, where they came from and how they evolved. *The Name Book* includes an insider's section on people who have entered the language as words, a name-dropper's list of those who have changed them and an invaluable pronunciation guide.

Guide to Wordplay and Word Games

From acrostics and alternades to word-chains and word squares, and having fun with spoonerisms, clerihews, limericks, Scrabble and the crossword on the way, this book explores the wit and wonder of word games.

The Secrets of Speed Reading

How fast do you read? Reading faster not only enables you to absorb more material in any given time, but also improves comprehension and enhances enjoyment. With *The Secrets of Speed Reading*'s proven technique and sequence of instruction, exercises and self-tests, you can reach double, even triple, your present speeds for your own benefit and satisfaction – at home, at work, or even on holiday.

A Full List of Titles Available from Mandarin in this series

While every effort is made to keep prices low, it is sometimes necessary to increase prices at short notice. Mandarin Paperbacks reserves the right to show new retail prices on covers which may differ from those previously advertised in the text or elsewhere.

The prices shown below were correct at the time of going to press.

☐	7493 1519 9	**Word Bank**	Graham King	£2.99
☐	7493 1520 2	**Good Grammar in One Hour**	Graham King	£2.99
☐	7493 1521 0	**Crisp Clear Writing in One Hour**	Graham King	£2.99
☐	7493 1522 9	**Word Check**	Graham King	£2.99
☐	7493 1523 7	**The Secrets of Speed Reading**	Graham King	£2.99
☐	7493 1524 5	**The Name Book**	Graham King	£2.99
☐	7493 1525 3	**Spell Check**	Graham King	£2.99
☐	7493 1526 1	**Guide to Word Play & Word Games**	Graham King	£2.99

All these books are available at your bookshop or newsagent, or can be ordered direct from the publisher. Just tick the titles you want and fill in the form below.

Mandarin Paperbacks, Cash Sales Department, PO Box 11, Falmouth, Cornwall TR10 9EN.

Please send cheque or postal order, no currency, for purchase price quoted and allow the following for postage and packing:

UK including BFPO
£1.00 for the first book, 50p for the second and 30p for each additional book ordered to a maximum charge of £3.00.

Overseas including Eire
£2 for the first book, £1.00 for the second and 50p for each additional book thereafter.

NAME (Block letters) ....

ADDRESS ....

....

☐ I enclose my remittance for ....

☐ I wish to pay by Access/Visa Card Number

Expiry Date